# TABLE OF CONTENTS

The sunlight is a kind of energy. It helps plants grow and warms the earth.

# A New True Book

# EXPERIMENTS WITH LIGHT

### By Ray Broekel

CHILDRENS PRESS®

CHICAGO

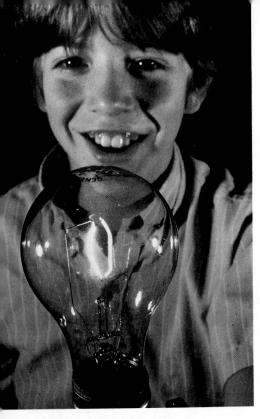

PHOTO CREDITS

Journalism Services:
© Joseph Jacobson — 4 (bottom left), 18, 45
© Harvey Moshman — 35 (left)
© Lee Starz — 15
© David Waselle — 14 (left)

Nawrocki Stock Photo:
© Robert Amft — Cover
© Michael Brohm — 7
© Candee — 29 (right)
© Rui Coutinho — 14 (right)
© Frank J. Neiman — 4 (top)
© Jim Wright — 2, 6 (2 photos), 11 (2 photos), 17, 20, 21, 24, 25, 27, 30, 35 (right), 36, 37 (2 photos), 38 (3 photos), 39, 40, 42, 43 (2 photos)

U.S. Naval Observatory — 13

© Jerome Wyckoff — 4 (bottom right), 29 (left), 33

© John G. Shedd Aquarium — 8

John Forsberg — 22

Light bulbs are luminous
because they give off light.

Library of Congress Cataloging-in-Publication Data

Broekel, Ray.
  Experiments with light.

  (A New true book)
  Includes index.
  Summary: A discussion of the nature and properties
of light, with experiments.
    1. Light—Experiments—Juvenile literature.
[1. Light—Experiments. 2. Experiments] I. Title.
QC360.B76  1986      535'.07'8      85-30888
ISBN 0-516-01278-9

# WHAT IS LIGHT?

One of your senses is the sense of sight. That sense, however, won't do much good unless light is present.

Light is a kind of energy. It makes things happen. It makes you able to see colors. It makes green plants manufacture food. It does other things, too.

# FROM WHERE DOES LIGHT COME ?

Stars give off light. Our sun is a star. Most of the light on earth comes from our sun.

But other things give off light, too. Fire gives off

The filament in a light bulb is made of metal. Electricity goes through and heats the filament. When the filament lights up it gives off light.

Close-up of hot molten metal

light. Bulbs give off light.

Objects that give off light are said to be luminous.

Metals give off light when they are made hot enough. The hot metals are then luminous.

Flashlight fish have lights. Pockets beneath each eye contain billions of bacteria that use sugar and oxygen from the fish's blood to make light.

Fireflies and some deep-sea fish give off a kind of light. These creatures have certain chemicals in their bodies that make this light. It is not hot.

# LIGHT CAN CHANGE INTO OTHER KINDS OF ENERGY

Light helps plants make their own food. The energy from the sunlight is changed into chemical energy and stored in the plant.

When light is absorbed, or taken in, it is changed into heat energy. Other kinds of energy changes take place, also.

# LIGHT RADIATES AND TRAVELS

Light is radiant energy. It goes out in all directions. The sun gives off radiant energy, so sunlight travels in all directions.

Light travels in straight lines. You can experiment to see this happen.

You will need two pieces of cardboard (about six inches square), a flashlight, and a darkened room.

Make a hole about the size of a pencil in the center of each cardboard. Place one cardboard

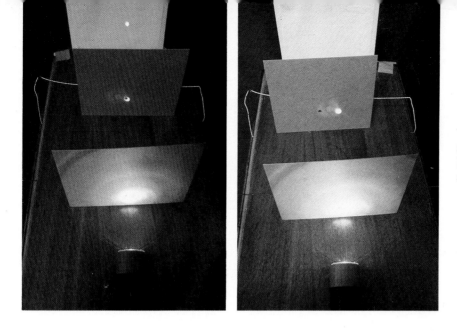

This experiment shows how light travels in straight lines.

several inches in front of the other.

Make sure the holes are in a straight line. Shine the flashlight at the first cardboard. If the two holes are in a straight line the light will shine onto the wall.

Now move one of the cardboards so the holes are no longer lined up.

Shine the flashlight again.

What happens?

No light will shine through onto the wall. When one of the holes is placed out of line, light no longer can get through.

# LIGHT TRAVELS LONG DISTANCES

Our sun is about 93 million miles away. It takes light a little over eight minutes to get to the earth after leaving the sun.

It takes about four years for the light from the next nearest star, Alpha Centauri, to reach the earth.

Other star groups are much farther away. The distances of these star

A spiral galaxy

groups, called galaxies, are measured in units called light years. A light year is the distance light travels in one year's time. It is equal to about six trillion miles.

Light travels through air at a speed of about 186,300 miles a second. Light does not travel with the same speed through

Light travels through water (above) faster than it does through glass (right).

all things. The speed of light through glass is about 124,000 miles a second. In water its speed is about 140,000 miles a second.

Lights of different colors also have different speeds. Blue light travels through glass faster than red light.

Light travels faster than sound. That is why you see a lightning flash before you hear the thunder it causes. It takes about one ten-thousandth of a second for the light from a lightning flash twenty miles away to reach your eyes.

# LIGHT CAN BE ABSORBED

Things that are light in color do not absorb as much light as dark-colored things. When things absorb light, the light will change into heat energy.

Wrap black paper or black cloth around one glass. Wrap the other glass with white paper or white cloth.

Fill both glasses with water and place them in a shady corner for half an hour. Now take the temperatures of the water in both glasses. The temperatures should be the same.

Place both glasses in sunlight for
half an hour. Check the temperatures
again. Now what do you notice?

The water temperature in the glass
wrapped in black should be higher.
This glass absorbed more of the light
than did the other one. The absorbed
light was transferred to the water.
And that light energy was changed
into heat energy.

Full moon

# MOONLIGHT IS REFLECTED SUNLIGHT

Our moon does not give off light of its own. Only the sun gives off light. When sunlight falls on the moon, some of that light is reflected to earth. We call it moonlight, but it really is reflected sunlight.

# LIGHT IS REFLECTED BY OBJECTS

Light is best reflected, or bounced off, when it falls on smooth, shiny objects. You can see things because of the light rays that are reflected into your eyes. A smooth surface, such as that of mirrors, reflects almost all the light that falls on it. These rays can be reflected over and over.

A mirror reflects images in reverse. That is, the left side of the object becomes the right side in the mirror.

Try the following. You will need three mirrors. Place one mirror in the path of some sunbeams. Put a second mirror in such a way that the light rays are reflected from the first mirror. Place the third mirror in the path of the reflected rays of the second mirror.

You can see the light because it has again been reflected. If you wish, you can keep placing mirror after mirror in the path of the light to keep reflecting it.

Young scientist observes how light is reflected at an angle

Light may be reflected from a mirror at an angle. Or it may be reflected straight forward. It all depends on how the light enters the mirror.

Light acts much like a bouncing ball. If you throw a ball straight down, it

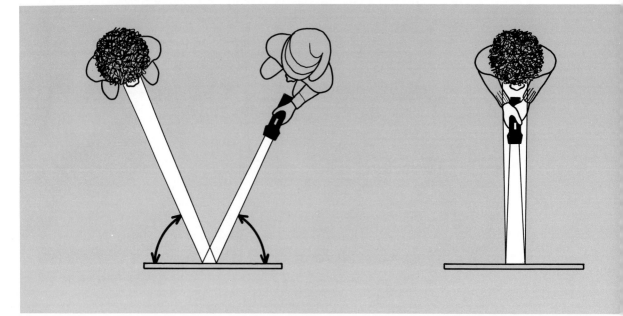

bounces straight back at
you. If you bounce the ball
at an angle, it bounces off
the floor at the same
angle away from you.

Try it with a ball. Light
will act the same way
when it is reflected.

# LIGHT CHANGES DIRECTION BY REFRACTION

Light almost always travels in a straight path. But it can be made to change direction. Light bends when it travels from one kind of matter to another. This bending of light is called refraction. When light travels from air into water, for example, refraction takes place.

Try this. Place a pencil in a glass of water. Look at it. Now place your finger in a glass of water. Look at it.

What happens to the pencil? Your finger? Did they really bend? No, they didn't change. They look changed because of the way the light was refracted.

When light rays pass from air into water, they slow down. And when light rays pass from water into

**WHEELS MAKE WORK EASIER**

Look at the two garbage cans shown in the pictures. Which can is easier to move? Try it and see.

EXPERIMENT

Use a pair of roller skates. Fasten a rubber band to each skate.

Hold one of the rubber bands and pull one skate with it lying on its side.

Hold skate on its and p kate needs the

H an you tell?

Refraction makes the words look larger and farther apart than they are.

air, those rays travel faster. Now what happens when light rays pass from glass into air?

You'll need a magnifying, or reading, glass to test this out. Look at two words on this page through the magnifying glass. How far apart do they seem to be? How far apart are they really? Refraction makes them look larger and farther apart than they really are.

Light does not travel at the same speed through all mediums. Air, water, and glass are three mediums.

Here's a chance to see how that works.

Put a coin at the inside bottom of a dish. Hold it in place with clay. Move back far enough so that the side of the dish hides most of the coin.

Now let a friend pour water into the dish. As water is placed in the dish the light bends. The coin seems to be rising.

You know the coin did not move. It just seems that way. This is a result of refraction. Light rays bend as they pass from one medium to another.

Young scientists demonstrate a refraction experiment.

# SEPARATING WHITE LIGHT

What is the color of
light? White. But that white
light is made up of
different colors. The colors
in a beam of white light
are violet, blue green,
yellow, orange, and red.

You can separate white
light into colors by using
a glass prism. As the white
light enters the prism,
its speed changes. The
change in speed causes the

Sunlight spectrum (left) from a prism.
Rainbow reflection from a laser disc (right).

beam of light to bend.

Each of the colors in the white light bends a different amount. Violet bends the most. Red light bends the least.

When the light leaves a prism there is a further bending of colors. This causes those different

29

White light breaks into different colors.

colors to spread out. You see what is called the whole spectrum of colors.

Try the following. Get a glass prism and a sheet of white paper. Darken the room by pulling all the shades except for one. Pull the shade almost all the way down. Hold the prism as shown in front of a stream of sunlight. You should see the white light broken up into different colors of the spectrum on the sheet of white paper.

# LIGHT RAYS
# CAN TRICK YOU

Look above a hot stove. When the heat rises, the hot air mixes with cooler air. The light that passes through the hot, then cool air, is refracted. So you see what appears to be the shimmer of light.

Cold air is denser than is warm air. So light is refracted as it passes from one to the other.

Light rays can trick you. A mirage sometimes can be seen during hot weather. You see what appears to be a body of water floating above the ground.

What you are seeing is caused by the refraction of light rays passing through layers of air having densities. In dense air the parts making up the air

These light rays are caused by the moisture and dust in the atmosphere.

are more tightly packed
than they are in less
dense air. So light traveling
through air of different
densities is refracted. Your
eyes are tricked by the
bending of light.

# COLOR IS IMPORTANT

Color helps you tell the difference between things that would otherwise look alike. For instance, some birds are almost the same size and shape. But you can tell them apart by their colors.

A dress that is green in color looks green. Why? Because the green dye in the dress absorbs all

Multicolored parrots (above) and the blue towel and green shirt (right), are examples of how different objects absorb color from white light.

the colors in white light except green. The green is reflected to your eyes, and you see the dress as green. A blue towel is blue because the dye in the towel absorbs all the other

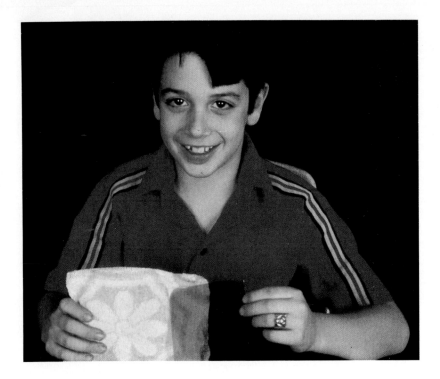

colors that are in white
light. The towel allows only
the light that causes a
blue color to remain.

Here's something to try. Hold blue
cellophane over a yellow towel. When
all the colors in white light are
absorbed, no color is left. What is
left is a shade of black. It is the
absence of color.

Taillights are good examples of
how colored filters affect white light.

What about traffic lights?
They are red, green, and
yellow. Each of those
traffic lights has a white
bulb behind. The *GO* light
has a green glass filter.
The *CAUTION* light has a
yellow glass filter. The
*STOP* light has a red filter.

Each of the glass filters absorbs all the other colors except for the one that needs to shine through. Where else can filters be used? Photographers use different colored filters on their cameras.

Colored filters (far right) are frequently used in photography. The girl (left) was photographed without a filter and then she was photographed using a blue filter.

Flashlight with
green cellophane

## EXPERIMENTING WITH COLOR

You will need a flashlight, a book, several pieces of cellophane in different colors, a darkened room, some rubber bands.

Shine the flashlight onto the pages of the book. Notice how bright the white light is on the page. Now use a rubber band to fasten a piece of colored cellophane in front of the flashlight. Shine the flashlight on the page again.

What have you done to the white light? You have caused the other colors in the white light to become absorbed. You have allowed only the color of the cellophane to get through. Try it again with another piece of colored cellophane. What happens?

Red cellophane allows only red to shine through.

# SOME LIGHT IS ABSORBED BY ALL THINGS

Some things allow little light to go through them. These things are opaque. Opaque things absorb almost all the light that shines on them.

Some objects allow more light to shine through. These objects are translucent. They absorb just some of the light that shines on them.

Transparent objects allow almost all the light that shines on them to get through. Very little of the light is absorbed.

Try this. Shine a light on the cover of a book. Does light show through on the other side? Why not? The book is opaque, so the light doesn't go through.

Books are opaque.

Frosted glass (left) is translucent. Clear glass (right) is transparent.

Shine a light on a piece of frosted glass. Does light show through on the other side? Some of it does? Why? Because the piece of frosted glass is translucent.

Now shine a light on a piece of clear glass. Does light show through on the other side? Most of it does because the piece of glass is transparent.

# THE SUN

Out in space there is stellar, or star, dust. As beams of light travel through space they may be absorbed by that stellar dust.

Your flashlight beam, since it is weak, would not travel very far in space. Only very strong beams of light, such as that given off by our sun, travel long

distances. The light from
other stars travels long
distances, too.

So thank goodness for
the sun. It lights and
heats our planet earth.

# WORDS YOU SHOULD KNOW

**electricity**(ih • lek • TRIH • sih • tee) — a property of matter in which some atomic particles attract and repel each other

**energy**(EN • er • gee) — the ability to do work

**filament**(FIL • ah • ment) — a fine wire used to produce light in an electric bulb

**filter**(FIL • ter) — a device that allows certain light rays to pass through it, while stopping others

**lightning**(LITE • ning) — a sudden flash of light caused by a discharge of electricty

**light year**(LITE YEER) — the distance light travels in one year — about six trillion miles

**particle**(PAR • tik • ihl) — a very small piece or part of something

**prism**(PRIZ • um) — a transparent glass object, triangular in shape, that can break up white light into the spectrum

**ray**(RAY) — a thin beam of light

**reflect**(ree • FLEKT) — to bounce off

**refract**(ree • FRAKT) — to cause a change in direction of a ray of light when passing from one medium to another

# INDEX

*About The Author*

*Ray Broekel is well known in the publishing field as a teacher,
editor, and author of science materials for young people. A full-time
freelance writer, Dr. Broekel has written many other kinds of books
for both children and adults. He has had over 150 published. He
also teaches several writing courses. Ray Broekel lives with his
wife, Peg, and a dog, Fergus, in Ipswich, Massachusetts.*